THE TREASON OF BENEDICT ARNOLD

Benedict Arnold was America's first traitor. Some two hundred years after the American Revolution, his name and deed are still synonymous with treachery and deceit. Yet few people today realize how close his treason came to succeeding; only the merest chance frustrated it. Had it been successful, the Revolution may well have sputtered and eventually died. In this account of Arnold's tragic story, the emphasis is on two themes: his secret dealings with the British; his skill as a military leader. Perhaps the outstanding battlefield officer — American or British — of the Revolutionary War, Arnold on two occasions (at Valcour Island and Bemis Heights) probably saved the young United States through his daring tactics, raw courage, and inspired leadership.

PRINCIPALS

Major General Benedict Arnold (1741-1801), the principal personality in the drama of his own treason, but there were others who played vital roles.

Major John André (1751-1780), British spymaster at No. 1 Broadway, New York, who corresponded with Arnold about the sale of West Point, the fortress on the Hudson that kept British armies in America and Canada apart.

General Sir Henry Clinton (1738-1795), who did not care to be Commander in Chief of the British army in America. Every few months he tried to resign. Then he saw a chance to end the American War "with one shining stroke," for the American general, Arnold, had showed the way.

General George Washington (1732-1795), who placed his trusted friend and subordinate, Benedict Arnold, in command of West Point. He would have preferred Arnold to lead an army, but the moody general complained that his wounds from Bemis Heights hadn't healed.

Benedict Arnold. *(American Antiquarian Society)*

A FOCUS BOOK

The Treason of Benedict Arnold 1780

An American General Becomes His Country's First Traitor

by Robert Kraske

FRANKLIN WATTS, INC.
575 Lexington Avenue   New York, N.Y. 10022

The authors and publisher of the Focus Books wish to acknowledge the helpful editorial suggestions of Professor Richard B. Morris.

Contents

General George Washington, as he appeared during the American Revolution. (Independence National Historical Park Collection)

Whom Can We Trust Now?

Monday, September 25, 1780.

With his servants and four aides, General George Washington rode along the river road toward West Point. Ahead trotted a guard of four light horsemen. A baggage cart rumbled behind. The morning was hazy with golden sunlight; autumn had changed the green of the Hudson River valley to bright red and gold.

The commander in chief was riding back from Hartford, Connecticut, where he had met with Count Rochambeau. The French commander did not have good news. A powerful English squadron held his six thousand French troops in a tight blockade at Narragansett Bay. Off France itself, more British warships prevented a second French army from leaving the port of Brest. Count Rochambeau was concerned; so far, the French had given the Americans little help in their fight for independence.

The year 1780 had brought Washington nothing but bad news. The winter at Morristown — far more severe than at Valley Forge — had almost finished his army. In order to get food, starving soldiers had hired out as farmhands. Throughout the Continental army, ammunition was low, and Washington had written to Congress of the "absolute emptiness of our magazines everywhere." In May, two Connecticut regiments had threatened mutiny. The same month saw the worst American defeat of the war. Charleston, South Carolina — the fourth largest city in the colonies — fell to the redcoats. A month later, a small British force routed General Horatio Gates's army of three thousand, leaving North Carolina and Virginia open to attack. And now, the threat of losing the entire South was imminent. Less than two weeks before, Admiral Sir George Rodney and ten ships of the line had arrived in New York Harbor. American spies reported that the ships were loading troops for a dash to the Chesapeake.

Nor were these the only concerns that burdened the American commander. The treasury was nearly empty; Congress no longer had the money to buy weapons, and the army had not been paid since January. Money was so scarce that Washington, on his trip to Hartford, was concerned that he could not pay for food and rooms for his staff. Congress had allowed him only eight thousand dollars for expenses. Fortunately, Governor Trumbull saved Washington from embarrassment. Connecticut, he declared tactfully, would be honored to pay the bills of General Washington and his staff.

The war had gone on now for five years and Washington had never wavered in his convictions. He firmly believed that, in time, America would win independence from Great Britain. But recently he had begun to have doubts. In June, he had written Congress a gloomy letter. Unless that body could muster the men, money, and energy to carry on the fight, "our cause is lost."

For the moment though, the tall, grave commander with the steady blue eyes and pockmarked cheeks put his doubts aside. The autumn morning was too fresh and ahead lay the pleasant prospect of breakfast with his old comrade Benedict Arnold and Arnold's twenty-year-old bride, Peggy. Washington had assigned his friend to the command of West Point less than eight weeks ago. He was eager to see the work Arnold had accomplished on the fort's defenses.

A Meeting with Benedict Arnold
at West Point

Located some fifty miles north of New York, the new fort was essential to America's defense. Twice during the past four years, columns of redcoats had moved south from Canada along the chain of rivers and lakes that ended with the Hudson River and New York City. Twice they had been defeated — victories for which General Arnold had been chiefly responsible. But now, with Fort Ticonderoga in upper New York State evacuated, the Americans had no defense along the upper Hudson but the three-year-old unfinished fortress at West Point. Without it, the colonies below were open to attack.

Suddenly Washington reigned in his horse. Before going on to Arnold's home and headquarters at Robinson House, he decided to inspect two redoubts — small earthwork fortifications — along the riverbank. He sent Majors Samuel Shaw and James McHenry ahead with the baggage cart to inform General Arnold that he would be delayed and to start breakfast without him. The Marquis de Lafayette and Colonel Alexander Hamilton followed as Washington eased his horse down a path to the river. An hour later, his inspection finished, Washington continued his ride toward Arnold's headquarters. Two servants dashed ahead, followed by the four cavalry guards, to tell Arnold that His Excellency would soon arrive.

Robinson House was located two and a half miles southwest of West Point on the east side of the Hudson. Set among apple and peach orchards, the house was surrounded on three sides by tree-covered hills.

[5]

Robinson House, Arnold's headquarters on the east bank of the Hudson River. (Library of Congress)

As Washington dismounted, he was surprised to learn that Arnold was not there. Arnold's secretary, David Franks, reported that the general had gone to West Point only a half hour before and would greet His Excellency there. Mrs. Arnold was also not present, Franks said. Although it was ten thirty in the morning, she had not as yet left her bedchamber.

Washington breakfasted, then took a boat across the Hudson to West Point. The senior officer on duty, Colonel Lamb, met Washington at the boat landing. He apologized for not having an honor guard ready, but he had no idea Washington planned to visit the fort.

Washington looked sharply at the man. Surely General Arnold had told him that the commander in chief would arrive soon. No, sir! The colonel had not seen General Arnold all morning.

That was not all that struck Washington as strange. As he walked about the grounds, he noticed only a handful of troops guarding the fort — and most of these were invalids, unable to put up a fight if they were called upon to do so.

Colonel Lamb explained that Arnold had ordered the troops out to cut wood. The nights were already chilly and the garrison would need enormous piles of firewood to survive the winter.

While this explanation was logical, it was really not satisfactory. Washington intended to speak to Arnold about not leaving an adequate guard force at the fort. There was always danger of a surprise attack.

[6]

Washington returned to Robinson House in midafternoon. His aide, Alexander Hamilton, was waiting with a packet of letters from Lieutenant Colonel John Jameson at North Castle. Jameson's letter explained that a "John Anderson" was being held prisoner. Anderson had a pass signed by General Arnold which allowed him to go through the lines to the British outpost at White Plains. Papers "of a very dangerous tendency," Jameson wrote, were found in Anderson's boots. He was enclosing these papers for Washington to examine.

Washington unfolded the papers — and was stunned. There in his hands lay the innermost secrets of the American high command: a copy of his last council of war and papers that detailed West Point's defenses — all in Arnold's handwriting.

A letter from "John Anderson" was also enclosed. His real name, Anderson admitted, was Major John André. He was adjutant general to Sir Henry Clinton, commander of British forces in America. His purpose in coming into the American lines was to meet a certain person and obtain military information. Because of events he could not control, he had been detained inside American lines and thus, to get back to New York, he "had to concert my escape."

Hamilton saw Washington's face flush with anger as the ugly truth sank home. Benedict Arnold — the man he had trusted with America's most valuable military stronghold — had sold out to the enemy!

Immediately, Washington sent Hamilton and another aide in pursuit of Arnold. But the shock was too much. Arnold, his friend, a traitor! He turned to the young Marquis de Lafayette. His hands trembled. "Arnold has betrayed us. Whom can we trust now?"

[7]

Arnold—"The Most Enterprising Man Among the Rebels"

The news of Benedict Arnold's treachery spread fast. Soldiers and civilians alike were shocked. "Treason of the blackest dye," wrote General Nathanael Greene in his orders of the day for September 26. Arnold's betrayal of West Point "must have given the American cause a deadly wound if not a fatal stab!"

Within a week, straw figures of Arnold were burned in Boston, Philadelphia, and Providence. In Norwich, Connecticut, where Arnold had been born thirty-nine years before, a furious mob stormed the town graveyard and destroyed the tombstone of Arnold's father simply because it bore the traitor's name.

Yet Arnold was no ordinary turncoat. During the war, many men, soldiers and civilians alike, changed sides and their doing so caused little comment. But Arnold was a national hero. Every regiment knew his name. Tory and Patriot households alike had often discussed his ingenious exploits. Even the British Parliament knew Benedict Arnold. Lord George Germain, secretary of state for the colonies, called him "the most enterprising man among the Rebels." Not only was this a generous tribute to an enemy, but it was one that was true; Arnold had been the outstanding battlefield officer, American or British, of the war.

What was extraordinary about Arnold was that he was not a professional soldier. Like most American generals of that day, he was an amateur. Yet he had an instinct for tactics, raw courage, and a remarkable talent for leading men. Years after the war, one veteran recalled: "He didn't care for nothing. He'd ride right in. It was, 'Come on, boys!' 'Twasn't, 'Go on, boys!' "

[8]

Arnold's military career began with the first American victory of the war. Leaving his profitable shipping business in New Haven — where he lived in a fine white house and kept two carriages and a stable of ten horses — he joined Ethan Allen in May of 1775 in a surprise raid on Fort Ticonderoga. The fort was located on a narrow channel that connected Lake Champlain to Lake George, two of the waterways the British would have to descend to invade the colonies from Canada. Oxen hauled the prize of fifty-nine brass cannon three hundred miles overland to Boston; the rebels were desperate for guns to defend the city.

With Ticonderoga under American control, Washington decided to end the threat of invasion from Canada with an attack on Quebec, the central storehouse in North America of British arms and supplies. His strategy looked sound — on paper. First, General Richard Montgomery would attack Montreal. Then, Montgomery would combine his army with one led by Arnold, and both armies would attack the walled city on the St. Lawrence.

Arnold's task was heroic. With eleven hundred men, he was to travel by *bateaux* — wooden boats with flat bottoms and tapered ends — three hundred fifty miles north through Maine and into Canada by the Kennebec, Dead, and Chaudiére rivers. The march was to last twenty days.

In high spirits, the troops left Cambridge at the end of September, but within two weeks they were in serious trouble. The clumsy four-hundred-pound bateaux were difficult to paddle and awkward to carry overland. The primitive maps of the day failed to show the boiling rapids or the portages around treacherous waterfalls. Muddy river water leaked into the boats and ruined the salt beef. The men drank river water and became sick with diarrhea. They slept in damp clothes and awoke in the morning with shirts and breeches "frozen a pane of glass thick," as one trooper recorded in his diary.

[9]

But the worst problem was hunger. Deer and birds fled before the troops crashing through the woods. By the end of October, the food was gone and the men were starving. Some cooked a gruel of shaving soap and barber's powder. Others roasted moose-hide breeches or boiled moccasins. A black dog, mascot of the expedition, fed a handful of men for one meal.

Arnold strode up and down the straggling column encouraging the men to push on. Finally, sick at the sight of so many lying down in the snow to await death, he pushed on alone.

Near the St. Lawrence, he was able to buy cattle, oatmeal, and flour from settlers and brought these supplies back to his starving troops — and just in time. The famished soldiers fell on the cattle, slaughtered them, and ate the flesh raw. By November 8, forty-six days after they had left Cambridge, the army arrived at the St. Lawrence, their survival due only to the courage and determination of their spirited commander.

But the British at Quebec refused to fight. As Arnold and Montgomery paraded their tattered troops in the snow before the gray walls, the British remained snug inside.

On the last day of the year, the two American commanders decided to attack. While this was not the best of plans, they had little choice; most of the men's enlistments ended at midnight. By the next day, they might not have men to command.

In a blinding snowstorm, covering gunlocks with coat lapels, the Americans headed for the city. The result was disastrous. A point-blank blast of grapeshot killed Montgomery and a dozen others. Moments later, Arnold himself went down when a ricocheting musket ball struck his left thigh. The Americans retreated. Their losses were 48 killed, 34 wounded, and 372 — a quarter of the total force — captured.

Arnold, now in sole command, maintained siege lines around Quebec until the spring sun melted ice in the St. Lawrence and British troop ships arrived. The Americans then retreated to Montreal and the redcoats followed. On June 18, 1776, Arnold and his men left Canada from St. John. Arnold was the last to leave. As a patrol of British cavalry came down the road, he put a bullet into his horse, placed his bridle and saddle into a canoe, and paddled away from shore. He took one honor with him: promotion to brigadier general from a grateful Congress.

The Battle of Lake Champlain

But Arnold's Canadian adventure was not finished. That summer, the British under Sir Guy Carleton planned an invasion of the colonies. At the northern end of Lake Champlain, they built a formidable fleet of frigates, flatboats, and gunboats. Seven hundred officers and men — including a regiment of tough blue-coated German mercenaries — prepared to sail south on the lake, subdue Fort Ticonderoga, and then continue down the Hudson to join General Sir William Howe in New York.

Opposing them were Arnold's ragtag veterans of Canada.

With the help of carpenters and ship's stores — canvas, anchors, hawsers, guns — hauled overland from New England, Arnold and his men built a tiny fleet of eleven ships. The ships were small and their armament light, just half the guns the British fleet could muster.

On September 23, Arnold took his fleet north on the lake and settled it behind Valcour Island. The 180-foot-high tree-covered island hid his ships from British scouts.

On October 11, as the British confidently sailed south, Arnold's little fleet dashed from behind the island. During a fierce seven-hour battle, the Americans lost the schooner *Royal Savage* and the gondola *Philadelphia*, but still managed to delay the British advance. Night, however, found the Americans at a serious disadvantage: the British squadron now stood between them and the southern end of the lake.

Arnold now did something the British hardly expected. Fog rolled over the lake that night. While carpenters busily repaired the British ships for the next day's fight, Arnold slipped his remaining nine ships single-file between the British and the shore. By morning, he had sailed his fleet eight miles down the lake.

This bold maneuver caught the British entirely by surprise. All day on October 12 they pursued the Americans. Caught on the thirteenth, Arnold lost eight ships, beached the last one, and escaped with his men through the woods to Fort Ticonderoga. The Americans now had nothing left to fight with; the fort and the colonies below were open to the British.

Then Carleton did a strange thing. Instead of pressing his advantage, he decided to return to Canada. Winter was coming on. The attack, he decided, could wait for better fighting weather in spring. Carleton did not realize it, but he had lost a chance to defeat the rebels and end the war. Arnold's delaying tactics in the three-day battle on Lake Champlain probably saved the young republic.

Arnold received well-earned praise for his skillful fight against Carleton's heavily armed fleet. British officers called him "a spirited fellow" for the way he had evaded capture. General Horatio Gates said: "Few men ever met with so many hairbreadth escapes in so short a time."

But there were critics, too, who saw only the loss of eleven ships. One of these critics was General William Maxwell. Writing to a friend from Ticonderoga, he called Arnold "our evil genius to the north," who "with a good deal of industry, got us clear of all our fine fleet. . . ."

However unjustified they might have been, these harsh words cut Arnold to the core. Despite all the praise he received, it was his nature to remember only the criticisms of jealous, small-minded men. It was a weakness that in time would have tragic results both for Arnold and for the United States.

The Second Invasion — Burgoyne Moves South

"This army must not retreat!" declared "Gentleman Johnny" Burgoyne, as he led seven thousand men on a second attempt to invade the colonies. An aristocrat, dashing and handsome, he rode to battle with cartloads of baggage including his private stock of wine. Burgoyne loved his comforts, but he was also a bold and talented soldier.

Down Lake Champlain his army came with 138 cannon in the late summer of 1777. Burgoyne placed a number of these guns on a bluff behind Fort Ticonderoga, and the Americans — shamefaced

[13]

*Major General Horatio Gates,
Arnold's commander at the Battle
of Saratoga. (Independence National Historical Park Collection)*

at their neglect of the heights — evacuated the fort without a fight. Now Burgoyne pressed on toward Albany, his faith in the superior fighting abilities of the British soldier fully justified. Only one obstacle stood in his way: an army commanded by Major General Horatio Gates.

"Granny Gates," his men called him, but not to his face. Fifty years old, round-shouldered, his spectacles often perched on the tip of his nose, Horatio Gates did not look it, but he was a tough, experienced soldier. He was also a very cautious one.

His strategy to halt Burgoyne was to build chest-high earthworks twenty-five miles north of Albany at Bemis Heights near Saratoga, tuck his men between cannon, and let Burgoyne attack.

His immediate subordinate was Brigadier General Benedict Arnold, who could not sit still for anything when a fight was brewing.

The first British attack came on September 19. Arnold, in defiance of Gates's orders, dashed in front of the earthworks and forced the redcoat infantry to retreat. Gates did not like this. He ordered Arnold to his headquarters tent at Freeman's Farm two miles to the rear.

Arnold refused to accept Gates's reprimand. He felt himself justified in attacking the British instead of defending the earthworks. He was also annoyed about something else. In his report to Congress, the older general had neglected to mention Arnold's successful attack. Perhaps Gates wanted credit for the victory all for himself!

Arnold's charge, while tactless, was probably true. Gates's temper flared and he removed Arnold from command, ordering him to stay in his tent at headquarters.

On October 7, Burgoyne attacked again. Unable to sit behind the lines and listen to the roar of cannon and the sharp crack of muskets, Arnold leaped on his bay mare and dashed into the center of the battle — again defying Gates's orders.

The troops cheered. "Now, come on, boys!" Arnold shouted, waving his sword. "If the day's long enough, we'll have them all in hell before night!"

Follow him the troops did. They stormed a key redoubt and forced the British to withdraw — but not before Arnold's horse fell dead under him and a musket ball crashed into his left leg, throwing him helpless to the ground.

Burgoyne retreated all the way to Saratoga where the pursuing Americans surrounded his army of fifty-nine hundred survivors and made them surrender.

It was an important victory. As a result of it, King Louis XVI

[15]

Painting depicts the wounding of Benedict Arnold during the storming of the redoubt at Saratoga. (Charles Phelps Cushing)

recognized the new republic and, on February 16, 1778, signed a treaty pledging France's aid in America's fight against Great Britain.

Two weeks after his surrender, Burgoyne sent a report to Sir Henry Clinton in Philadelphia. Arnold was the American officer primarily responsible for his army's defeat, he told Clinton. "It was his doing!"

[16]

But the hero of Bemis Heights was unaware of this. Arnold lay in a hospital bed in Albany, his left leg crippled. On May 1, he went home to New Haven and was welcomed by a parade of soldiers and a thirteen-gun salute. Washington sent him a set of epaulets and sword knots — an exceptional compliment. But Arnold brooded over his crippled leg. Where could an invalid warrior serve? He was no longer fit for combat.

For the present, Washington decided to retire him. He assigned Arnold to the military command of Philadelphia which the British had evacuated in June, 1778.

The assignment was a grave error. From now on, this aggressive general would fight his battles with civilians.

Trials in Philadelphia

When Arnold arrived in Philadelphia on June 19, 1778, his mind was occupied by a private matter: he wanted to make his fortune. This was not unusual, for many men in high places during the Revolutionary War used their positions to turn a profit for themselves.

What was unusual, however, was the speed with which Arnold began looking for moneymaking opportunities. Four days after his arrival at headquarters in the John Penn mansion on Market Street, he had contacted General James Mease, in charge of army supplies for the Continental army. The two entered into a secret arrangement to use army money to buy up great quantities of goods — far more than the army needed — then sell the surplus to civilians for their own profit.

Nor was this the only illegal scheme Arnold entered into. A few months later, he authorized the use of twelve army wagons to unload a cargo of linens, glass, sugar, tea, and nails from a schooner in Boston Harbor for sale in private stores. Arnold received half the profits for allowing his partners to use the wagons.

In Philadelphia, Arnold lived lavishly and his expenses ran high. Although his army pay came to only $332 per month, he drove around town in a coach with four footmen, entertained with dinners served on fine china, and frequently attended plays at the Old Southwark Theater.

When his daily expenses amounted to more than his income, he tried to borrow money from the French minister in Philadelphia. The Chevalier de la Luzerne politely but firmly refused.

Soon Arnold's expensive habits caught the eyes of patriots on the Council of Pennsylvania. The war, they felt, demanded personal sacrifices and a modest manner of living. When they saw Arnold entertaining the wives of wealthy loyalists in his grand home, they began to criticize him openly. Nor did Arnold help the situation with his arrogant reply: "I have not yet learned to carry on warfare against women!"

The council was made up of powerful men and they had come to dislike Arnold. They demanded that Congress remove him from Philadelphia. Arnold, they charged, was acting in a manner improper to his high station. Moreover, they had found out about his use of army wagons for personal profit. He had also given too many passes to people traveling to British-held New York.

The charges were minor . . . the council did not know about his other moneymaking activities. Congress took a whole year to debate the matter, and finally decided that Washington should reprimand him for "imprudent and improper" use of the wagons.

Considering what the council had missed in its investigation of his affairs, Arnold should have considered himself fortunate. A reprimand from the commander in chief was light enough punishment. But Arnold decided not to submit to it. In wildly emotional letters to Washington, he defended his honor, listed his many services to his country, and reminded Washington that he, Arnold, had become crippled in the cause of independence. The council was persecuting him; he was innocent.

Washington tried to soothe his wounded feelings, but he could do only as Congress ordered. His reprimand was mild enough, but Arnold's pride was deeply hurt.

Nor was this the only injustice Arnold suffered from Congress — or so he felt.

There was the matter of expense money for the Canadian expedition. Congress had authorized Arnold $66,671. By the time he returned to the colonies, he could not account for $55,000 of the money. Arnold explained that he had lost his account books at the battle of Valcour Island.

Congress, however, was not satisfied with this explanation. Some critics even suggested that Arnold had used the missing money for his own use.

But it was still another matter that caused Arnold the most concern. On February 19, 1777, Congress promoted five brigadier generals to major general. Arnold was not among those promoted. He appealed to Washington for an explanation. The denial of promotion, he said, was "an implied impeachment of my character."

Washington wrote to Richard Henry Lee, a member of Congress. "Surely a more active, a more spirited, and sensible officer fills

[19]

no department in your army." Why, he asked, was Arnold passed over for promotion?

Lee wrote back, saying that Arnold's home state, Connecticut, already had two major generals. Congress did not want to appoint another major general from that state. Moreover, other states wanted major generals, too, and there were only so many commissions to go around.

Washington sent the reply on to Arnold, adding that, "I confess this is a strange mode of reasoning."

Arnold thought so, too. He decided to journey to Philadelphia and present his case directly to Congress.

On the way south, he ran into a British attack at Danbury, Connecticut. Arnold immediately took charge. With only five hundred half-trained militia to battle two thousand British regulars, he harrassed the redcoats all the way back to their ships on Long Island Sound. One horse was shot dead under him, a second wounded, and he himself took a bullet through his coat collar.

Congress could not help but be impressed. As a reward, it presented him with a horse, bridle and saddle, and, on May 12, promoted him to major general.

But Arnold never forgot Congress's former slight. He felt that body had treated him shabbily. Other, less capable men were handed promotions, but he had to risk his life to win his. The injustice of the whole matter rankled deep within Arnold.

Despite his troubles with Congress and the Council of Pennsylvania, one note of happiness came to Arnold during his days in Philadelphia. He met, courted, and won the hand of Peggy Shippen, a pretty brown-haired girl from one of Philadelphia's leading families.

Peggy lived in a large house on Fourth Street. During the Brit-

I *Benedict Arnold Major General* do acknowledge the UNITED STATES of AME-RICA to be Free, Independent and Sovereign States, and declare that the people thereof owe no allegiance or obedience to George the Third, King of Great-Britain; and I renounce, refuſe and abjure any allegiance or obedience to him; and I do *Swear* that I will, to the utmoſt of my power, ſupport, maintain and defend the ſaid United States againſt the ſaid King George the Third, his heirs and ſucceſſors, and his or their abetors, aſſiſtants and adherents, and will ſerve the ſaid United States in the office of *Major General* which I now hold, with fidelity, according to the beſt of my ſkill and underſtanding.

Sworn before me this 30th May 1778 at the Artillery Park Valley Forge

B Arnold

Arnold's oath of allegiance to the United States, signed at Valley Forge, May 30, 1778. (National Archives)

ish occupation, she and two sisters entertained British officers in their home. One of these officers was a Captain John André, a handsome young man with polished manners who flattered the winsome girl by drawing sketches of her.

In March, 1779, Arnold bought Mount Pleasant, a ninety-six-acre estate on the Schuylkill River. The following month, he and the eighteen-year old Peggy were married. At the ceremony, a soldier stood at Arnold's side to support him. Later, Arnold sat in a chair, his injured leg supported on a camp stool, to accept the good wishes of the wedding guests.

Arnold's marriage was a turning point in his life. He had attained something he had always wanted: social position and respect-

Mount Pleasant mansion, once the home of Benedict Arnold and his wife, as it looks today in Fairmount Park, Philadelphia. (Charles Phelps Cushing)

A portrait of Peggy Shippen (Mrs. Benedict Arnold) and her child. (Charles Phelps Cushing)

ability. In pursuing his personal goals, his allegiance to the revolution seems to have waned. What, after all, was independence? If it meant being subjugated to the rule and whims of petty men in high offices, he wanted none of it. The British, he may have concluded, were a far finer breed of men.

Peggy probably encouraged him in this attitude. She remembered the courtly British officers who came to her home on Fourth Street. But exactly what influence she had on Arnold's decision to join the British is not known. She shared her husband's secret thoughts though — that much is obvious. A month after their marriage, Arnold opened negotiations with the British for his services.

A Plan to Capture West Point

May 10, 1779.

On this bright spring day, a man named Joseph Stansbury arrived in New York and went directly to British headquarters in the Archibald Kennedy mansion at No. 1 Broadway.

Stansbury was the owner of a glass and china shop on Front Street in Philadelphia. He was also a loyalist who was against separation from England. But except for circulating some humorous verses about the rebels and joining with friends to sing "God Save the King" behind the locked and shuttered doors of his shop, he gave the Americans in Philadelphia no trouble.

Ushered into the presence of Sir Henry Clinton's adjutant general, Major John André, he told the young officer in the bright

scarlet uniform that he had come to speak for a certain gentleman high in the American military command.

This gentleman, said Stansbury, was considering offering his services to Sir Henry, but he wanted to be certain of one thing: that the British had no plan to quit the war and concede independence to the Americans.

André was in charge of British intelligence. Stansbury's offer did not especially interest him. So an unknown American officer wanted to reestablish his allegiance to the Crown! There was nothing unusual in this; every day, scores of rebels came back to the fold.

If Stansbury wished, said André, he might inform this gentleman that England had no intention, in any case, of giving up the war. But if he had information of military value to communicate, he would be amply rewarded.

André then told Stansbury about the code to use to send information through the lines. The unknown gentleman should use one of two books, Bailey's *Dictionary* or Blackstone's *Commentaries*. He should use three numbers to make up each word. The first number would be the page, the second number the line, and the third number would be the position of the word on the line. An "A" in the corner of a letter would mean that acid had been used to write a message in invisible ink between the lines of an ordinary letter; heat would make the message emerge.

At 29, John André was a five-year veteran of the war. Captured in Canada by the Americans in 1775, he spent a year in a prison camp in Pennsylvania. Released in an exchange of prisonors, André became aide-de-camp to Major General Charles Grey. In 1777, he took part in the infamous Paoli Massacre, in which British infantry, flints removed from their muskets, attacked a regiment of Americans at night and killed two hundred men with their bayonets only.

But André had no real heart for combat. He wangled an appointment as aide to Sir William Howe in Philadelphia and spent a year in such gentle and unwarlike pursuits as writing plays, designing costumes, and stage scenery, and practicing his charms on the daughters of Philadelphia's loyalists.

When Sir Henry Clinton became British commander in chief, André flattered the lonely and unpopular general and, perhaps to no one's surprise, became the general's favorite aide. Veteran officers suddenly found their orders from Clinton coming through this young man. He was fast becoming a power in the army and he was ambitious. Accordingly, Major André was treated with caution and respect.

Two weeks after his interview with Stansbury, André received the first coded message from Arnold. "General Washington and

[25]

A man of many talents, Major John André drew these portraits of himself. (Left, Charles Phelps Cushing; below, Yale University Library)

the army move to the North River [the Hudson] as soon as forage can be obtained. Congress have given up Charles Town if attempted. They are in want of arms, ammunition, and men to defend it. . . ."

Arnold concluded his message with a businesslike inquiry about payment for his "risk and service." He bluntly asked: "Inform me what I may expect."

But neither Clinton nor André thought too much of the intelligence Arnold offered. Besides, André's own agents had already sent the same information. What it came down to was that, as military governor of Philadelphia, Arnold had little military information to sell, yet he demanded a high price for his services.

At the end of July, Clinton wrote to Arnold with a direct suggestion for earning money: "Join the army, accept a command, be surprised, be cut off. . . . A complete service of this nature involving a corps of five or six thousand men would be rewarded with twice as many thousand guineas."

A few days later, André sent a message that urged the same: "Procure an accurate plan of West Point, or Washington's headquarters near Newburgh."

Through October, André kept getting messages from Arnold, but the information was still too general to be of real value. André refused to make a definite offer until Arnold came up with something the British could use. This hurt the moody Arnold; his services were not as valuable as he had imagined.

Fall and winter passed and André received no more messages from Arnold. Sometime during these months, Arnold resigned the command of Philadelphia and retired to his estate on the Schuylkill. Little is known of this brief period in Arnold's life, but from what happened later it is certain that he was brooding over ways to make his services more valuable to the British.

Arnold's coded letter to Clinton in which he offered West Point for 20,000 British pounds. (William L. Clements Library, University of Michigan)

In June, André suddenly heard from Arnold again. He reported on French troop ships about to arrive off Rhode Island in July. He also enclosed information about West Point. After an inspection trip to the fort, he reported that the garrison had only a ten-day supply of food. He also outlined places where the British could locate cannon for an attack on the fort. His final comment was about the vital chain stretched across the Hudson that the fort guarded:

"I am convinced the boom or chain across the river to stop the shipping cannot be depended on. A single ship, large and heavy-loaded with a strong wind and tide, would break the chain."

This was the kind of information André was looking for. What agent of their own could duplicate it? Then, in late July, he received a message that must have made his heart skip a beat. The possibilities were simply incredible and added up to nothing less than a chance to win the war. "If I point out a plan of co-operation," Arnold wrote, "by which Sir Henry shall possess himself of West Point, the garrison, etc., etc., etc., £20,000 sterling I think will be a cheap purchase for an object of so much importance."

André's agents reported that Arnold had taken command of West Point in early August. Now the American general was putting the fort up for sale! The prospect dazzled the young major.

Yet Sir Henry was suspicious. The offer was almost too good. Perhaps West Point was being offered as bait to lead the British into a disastrous trap. Was their correspondent really General Arnold? Or had the letters really come from Washington's intelligence chiefs as part of an elaborate plot to trick the British?

Before Clinton would commit a British army, someone had to talk with Arnold face to face. The only question was: Who.

The bright, eager face of his young aide beamed. What an op-

Arnold's coded note to Sir Henry Clinton in which he informed on Washington. The decoded note reads: "General Washington will be at King's Ferry Sunday Evening next on his way to Hartford, where he is to meet the French Admiral and General and will lodge at Peak's Kill." (William L. Clements Library, University of Michigan)

portunity for glory, perhaps even a title! Clinton agreed. André should be the one to contact Arnold and to work out details for the British attack on the fort.

But Arnold was not done sending information; he had one more piece of intelligence to report. Washington, he wrote, would be crossing the Hudson at King's Ferry, about thirteen miles below West Point, on Sunday, September 17, on his way up to Hartford to meet Count Rochambeau. He would stay the night at Peekskill. A sudden raid by the British might result in his capture.

Thus, as Arnold prepared to quit the American cause, did he give a final thought to the man who, more than any other over the past five years, had been his friend, supporter, and admirer. As it turned out, the British did not attempt this raid. Arnold's letter had arrived too late.

The Key to the War

Despite their political differences, Washington and Sir Henry Clinton saw eye to eye on one aspect of the war: the strategic value of West Point.

Washington called it "the key to America." Clinton saw the Hudson River (it was then called the North River) and Lake George and Lake Champlain to the north as a water highway down which troops and ships from Canada could descend and overwhelm the colonies.

The key to the war, both men believed, was control of the

[31]

West Point about 1783. The bend of the Hudson is visible at left. The great chain, designed to prevent the passage of enemy vessels, stretches across the river from in front of the tree in the foreground to the rocks below the fort in the background. (U.S. Military Academy Museum)

Hudson. For Washington, the broad river was a lifeline for troops and supplies, a communication route between the New England colonies and those to the south.

For Clinton, control of the Hudson meant cutting the United States in two and forcing Washington's troops into the rugged back-country where they would be rendered useless as a fighting force. With the British in control of major cities and forts in the colonies, the flame of the revolution would sputter and die.

In 1775, Congress had ordered a survey of the Hudson for the purpose of setting up a series of forts. The survey showed that only two natural sites for forts existed along the river: at Ticonderoga and West Point.

[32]

At West Point, the Hudson made a sharp bend and narrowed to a mere fifteen hundred feet. It was the strongest defensive position on the river. At low tide, mud flats and rocks appeared on the river bottom. For sailing ships to ease around the bend, even at high tide with a favorable wind, took considerable skill on the part of a captain. Guns positioned at the bend would make the passage extremely hazardous if not downright impossible.

In 1778, Washington assigned a fiery-tempered Scotsman, General Alexander McDougall, and a Polish engineer, Thaddeus Kosciusko, to build the fort. It was to be constructed on the west side of the Hudson on a high plain that plunged abruptly to the river.

The first piece of construction was a great chain forged at the Sterling Iron Works near West Point. Composed of nearly 1,000 massive links weighing 114 pounds each, the chain stretched 1,700 feet between the riverbanks. It cost $2,000 per ton.

In April, 1778, this chain was mounted on log floats and drawn across the Hudson. The ends were bolted into rocks on shore. In front of the chain floated a boom of logs lashed together and anchored to the river bottom. The purpose of the boom was to cushion the shock of a ship attempting to ram the chain. When Arnold saw the chain in 1780, the logs were water-soaked and decaying. He concluded that a heavily loaded ship sailing with the wind and tide could smash through it.

With the huge chain in place, McDougall and Kosciusko began constructing three forts on the plain above the river. Cannon in these forts were aimed directly at the chain.

The two engineers worked hard with the men and money appropriated by Congress for the fort. But by the time Arnold took command on August 3, 1780, it was still only partially finished. As Arnold correctly noted on his inspection trip earlier that summer,

[33]

the fort was open to attack at any number of points. If troops quartered there could be sent away on daily woodcutting details, the fort could be made even more vulnerable.

The British attack had to succeed; nothing could be left to chance. For Arnold, too much was at stake for any other outcome. He was relieved, therefore, when a note came from André suggesting a meeting.

The Meeting in the Fir Trees

The meeting between Arnold and André took place on the night of September 21-22. On that last night before he left New York, André had been guest of honor at a dinner given by Sir Henry. Raising his glass, the short and paunchy British commander toasted his young aide: "And when he returns, his efforts crowned with success, 'sir' shall be added to his name!"

Admiral Sir George Rodney's ships of the line were waiting in the harbor for the dash up the Hudson. To keep their true destination a secret, Sir Henry had leaked word that they were headed for Chesapeake Bay. Everything was ready; all awaited André's return.

At Dobbs Ferry just inside British lines, André boarded a small sloop and sped north up the Hudson. Near Teller's Point, he transferred to the larger sloop of war *Vulture*, anchored in midstream. There he waited word from Arnold.

Shortly after midnight, a longboat bumped alongside. Seated

in the stern was Joshua Hett Smith. A wealthy landowner on Haverstraw Bay and the younger brother of William Smith, royal chief justice of New York, Smith was suspected by the Americans of having Tory leanings. Learning this when he arrived to take command of West Point, Arnold cultivated Smith and then entrusted him with the mission of escorting André ashore.

Smith relished the intrigue of a midnight mission to pick up Arnold's agent. If he was surprised to find André dressed in the scarlet uniform of a British officer, he said nothing. Arnold had hinted vaguely that his meeting with the man had something to do with arranging peace terms between America and England.

The longboat grated on the western shore of the Hudson about two o'clock and the two oarsmen — tenant farmers on Smith's land — promptly went to sleep. Smith climbed the bank, found Arnold in a grove of fir trees, and hissed for André to join them. Then, much to Smith's surprise, Arnold dismissed him. Smith protested, but Arnold overrode his objections. The plump young man spent the rest of the night in the longboat.

For the next two hours, Arnold and André sat with their backs against a fir tree and talked. No one knows to this day what their conversation was about, but reasonable guesses can be made. Arnold undoubtedly wanted guarantees that his price for West Point would be paid. For his part, André wanted assurance that the Americans were not arranging a clever trap for the British when they approached the fortress. How to coordinate the British attack with the existing American defenses was another question.

On and on they talked until they heard a cautious whisper: "Gentlemen! It's time!" Smith was eager to return André to the *Vulture* before morning. The east bank of the Hudson was already edged with gray light.

The nocturnal meeting between General Arnold and Major André. H.M.S. Vulture *lies at anchor in the Hudson awaiting André's return. (Charles Phelps Cushing)*

But too many details were still unsettled. André was not yet ready to leave. Then Arnold decided to continue the conversation at Smith's house. André could return to the *Vulture* on the following night.

Smith lived only a few miles up the river road in a handsome stone house. Here the Hudson was four miles wide. From the second-story bedroom, André could see a comforting sight — HMS *Vulture* waiting for him on the peaceful river.

While Smith prepared breakfast — he had sent his family to relatives in Fishkill — the two conspirators continued their conversation.

Arnold produced a packet of secret papers, possibly to convince André of his sincerity. The papers were all highly damaging to the rebel cause. One described the unfinished condition of West Point: "Redoubt No. 3, a slight Wood Work 3 Feet thick, very Dry, no Bomb Proofs . . . easily set on fire — no cannon," and so on. Another document revealed the disposition of the troops at the fort. Yet another was a copy of Washington's last Council of War which described help expected from France and included a plan for a diversionary attack on British-held Jamaica to ease pressure on the colonies.

As the two men discussed the papers, the sharp report of a cannon broke the morning quiet. Startled, they rushed to a window and saw puffs of smoke bursting from the battery on Teller's Point. The four-pounder and howitzer were firing on the *Vulture*. Before the British sloop raised sail and headed downriver, six balls pierced her hull.

At the sight of the disappearing sail, André must have felt profound despair. Arnold, however, met the crisis with his usual daring.

Benedict Arnold's pass, given to Major André. (Charles Phelps Cushing)

If André could not return to New York by water, well, then, he could go by land — and Smith would escort him.

Sitting at the table, Arnold wrote out three passes. The first gave Smith permission for a boat if, on the way to New York, they met *Vulture* on the river. The second allowed Smith to go to White Plains — the northernmost British outpost — and return afterward. André's pass read: "Permit Mr. John Anderson to pass the guard to the White Plains or below, if he chooses, he being on public business by my direction." He signed each pass: "B. Arnold, M Genl."

Arnold left Smith's house at ten o'clock for West Point. But before leaving, he insisted that André conceal the secret papers in his boots. André spent a restless afternoon. Smith saw him go to the roof and scan the empty river, then return to the second-floor bedroom and resume pacing.

Toward sunset, Smith and André mounted horses and started

on the long journey southward to the British lines. Since they would be passing American guard posts, Smith suggested that André exchange his scarlet uniform coat for one of Smith's civilian coats. Over Smith's coat, André wore his heavy cape buttoned to the neck. He kept his boots, breeches, and waistcoat on, since these would not identify him as a British officer.

At King's Ferry, they crossed in a longboat to the east bank of the Hudson. While waiting for the ferry, Smith stopped at a guard's tent for a bowl of punch. In a loud, self-important voice, he informed all who would listen that he was on a mission of great importance.

A representation of Arnold persuading André to conceal the secret papers in his boots. (Charles Phelps Cushing)

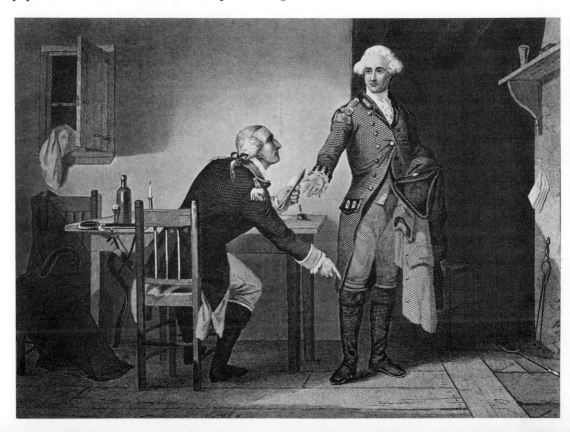

The guards all knew Smith; they laughed. No one really believed him.

André was silent as they mounted horses again across the Hudson. But Smith insisted on stopping again. While André waited on the road, his chin buried in his cape, Smith boasted to Colonel James Livingston that he was escorting a gentleman on a secret mission for General Arnold. Livingston was impressed and invited Smith and his mysterious companion for dinner. To André's relief, Smith declined; the importance of their mission, he informed Livingston, demanded all haste.

They cantered another six miles along the road. Smith chattered on, but André said nothing. The evening light was fading. Suddenly a sentry stepped onto the road. "Halt!" Behind him appeared Captain Ebenezer Boyd holding a lantern and demanding their passes.

When Smith told him they were bound for White Plains, Boyd warned that travel at night was unsafe. Bands of British and American deserters — "irregulars" he called them — roamed the countryside between the Croton River and White Plains. These irregulars scratched a living by looting farms and robbing travelers. The situation had become so bad that farmers stood guard at night while their families hid in wheat cricks and haystacks. Boyd suggested that Smith and his companion spend the night in a nearby farmhouse.

Smith and André slept in the same bed. André did not remove his boots. After a restless night, he was up at first light and eager to be on the road. With luck, they could be in White Plains by noon.

At the Croton River, they stopped at a farmhouse for breakfast. The Dutch housewife apologized; only last night, she said, a band of looters had crossed the river and stripped her cupboards. She could offer them only *soupaan* — a porridge of Indian meal and water.

Hearing this news, Smith decided to turn back; British irregulars across the river might just give him trouble. Besides, his family at Fishkill was waiting. He made André promise to return his bridle and saddle — the horse belonged to Arnold. André courteously offered his gold watch as security, but Smith refused it.

Breakfast over, Smith mounted and departed northward along the road they had come by. Later, on his way to Fishkill that afternoon, he reported to Arnold that André had passed safely through the lines to White Plains.

Now alone, André prepared to cross Pine's Bridge over the Croton, the southern boundary of the American lines. Ahead stretched a mere fifteen miles of neutral ground before he came to the British outpost at White Plains. His pass from Arnold would protect him from American irregulars; and if he met British deserters, well and good. His true identity would see him safely through.

He alternately jogged his horse and walked it. The morning was sunny and the trees blazed with red and gold. Saturday, September 23, was the second day of autumn.

Confusion at North Castle

A half-mile north of Tarrytown, three men lay playing cards in the bushes alongside Hardscrabble Road. The three were dressed roughly in leather breeches, checked shirts, coarse flannel jackets, and rawhide shoes. Their leader, John Paulding, wore a blue coat that had once belonged to a German soldier in the ranks of the British.

Paulding, Isaac Van Wart, and David Williams were American deserters living in the no-man's-land between White Plains and the Croton River — three of the many notorious "irregulars" that Captain Boyd had mentioned to André and Smith the night before. This morning they hoped to take a few head of cattle being driven on the road to New York. Cattle would be a rich prize for a lazy morning's work. But it was almost ten o'clock and they still had not taken a single prize.

Then Paulding, looking up from his cards, saw a lone rider on a fine chestnut stallion coming along the road. The horseman crossed a bridge over a narrow stream and began climbing the low hill that would bring him directly alongside.

As the rider approached the crest of the hill, Paulding stepped out of the bushes and pressed the muzzle of his musket against the man's chest. Startled, the rider reined in his horse.

Surveying the three, John André said, "Gentlemen, I hope you belong to our party?" He had noticed Paulding's Hessian coat.

"What party might that be?" Paulding asked.

"The lower party."

"We do."

André sighed. "Thank God, I am once more among friends!" He declared himself a British officer on a secret mission behind American lines. To prove his identity, he brought out his gold watch. All British officers carried such watches.

Paulding grabbed the watch and ordered André off his horse. They were not really of the "lower party" in New York, he said. They were Americans. His Hessian coat? He had used it as a disguise to escape only three days before from the Sugar House, the British prison in New York.

André laughed lightly. "God bless my soul!" he said. "A body must do anything to get along nowadays."

He reached into his coat and pulled out Arnold's pass. Pretending now to be an American himself, André said that he was on his way to Dobbs Ferry to obtain important intelligence for General Arnold. It would be wise, André suggested, not to delay him on his mission.

Paulding was the only one of the three who could read. The pass was genuine, he could see that. Van Wart and Williams urged letting the horseman go. They did not want trouble with General Arnold.

But Paulding was suspicious, and probably just a little disappointed; the only prize of the morning was about to ride away — free. A fine gentleman like this must have a little money on him to make their morning more profitable. He ordered Van Wart and Williams to search the saddlebags while he conducted André off the road and into the bushes. He held his musket ready as André stripped.

But there was no money in the saddlebags and none on André's person. Still, the three irregulars were not satisfied. Someone said, "He must have it in his boots."

Paulding found the papers.

André watched them closely. The three looked confused. The pass from Arnold was genuine enough, but the papers — all about West Point, they saw — suggested their prisoner might have stolen them and was now headed for New York to turn them over to the British.

"Gentlemen," André said, trying to resolve their confusion, "I

[43]

A Currier & Ives version, nearly a century after the event, of the capture of John André. The secret papers have been removed from André's boots as he offers his gold watch to one of his captors. (Library of Congress)

believe we can reach some agreement. What would you say to ten thousand guineas?"

Their whiskered jaws dropped. A bribe to let him go! Did he have the money now? No, it would have to be delivered to them after he reached New York. What guarantee could he give? His word of honor.

Monument at the spot where Major André was captured in North Tarrytown. (Charles Phelps Cushing)

Historical marker showing spot where Major André was captured in North Tarrytown. (Charles Phelps Cushing)

The proposition was simply too grand — ten thousand guineas! They decided on the spot that this fine gentleman must be a cheat. Once they let him go, he would never pay the money.

Ordering André to dress and mount, they took the bridle and ran along back roads and across fields to the nearest American outpost at North Castle.

Only once did André speak. "I would to God you had blown my brains out when you stopped me," he muttered.

Lieutenant Colonel John Jameson was in charge of the cavalry post at North Castle. He was new at his job. When Paulding, Van Wart, and Williams came into camp with André, he did not really know what to do. André took advantage of his confusion by insisting on writing a note to Arnold saying he was being detained on the general's business at North Castle. Arnold would hardly like that, he told the American officer.

Jameson was befuddled. He knew Arnold was expecting a John

[46]

Anderson from New York — all the posts on the east side of the Hudson had been alerted to look out for him — but this situation was different. Anderson had been delivered by three ruffians, he was bearing a pass from Arnold, and he was now going in the opposite direction — and with those damaging papers about West Point.

Not exactly sure what to do, Jameson decided to send André, escorted by two guards, back to Arnold at West Point. He gave one guard a letter to Arnold explaining André's capture. The letter also informed Arnold that he was sending the papers by another rider to General Washington at Hartford.

With André gone and the papers sent off by another rider, Jameson felt relieved. He had performed his duty to the best of his ability. Paulding, Van Wart, and Williams also left. They kept André's watch and his fine horse, saddle, and bridle as a reward for their morning's work.

But the matter was not yet finished. A few hours after André left, Major Benjamin Tallmadge rode into camp. Tallmadge was Washington's intelligence chief.

When Jameson told him about André and the papers, Tallmadge immediately became suspicious. The papers, he declared, showed that Arnold was selling out to the British and the "John Anderson" was the messenger between Arnold and the redcoats.

(This was a serious charge to make against the commanding general of the military district, but Tallmadge had some reason for making it. American agents in New York had heard rumors of an unidentified high-ranking American officer who was dealing with the British. Tallmadge now believed Arnold was that officer.)

Tallmadge also realized that, when Anderson was delivered to Arnold, both of them would naturally make their escape. Therefore, he urged Jameson to send a rider after Anderson and his guards and order them to return to North Castle.

Fortunately, the rider caught up with the group near Peekskill and, by Sunday morning, André was back at North Castle.

But Jameson was still uncertain. He was not as convinced as Tallmadge that Arnold was a traitor. There must be a better explanation of the whole matter. He agreed to hold Anderson a prisoner, but insisted on sending his original letter to Arnold. Lieutenant Solomon Allen placed the letter in his saddlebag and left for West Point.

After Allen had gone, the messenger who was taking Jameson's letter and the packet of secret papers to Washington rode back into camp. The commander in chief, he reported, was no longer at Hartford. He was on his way to West Point, but no one knew which route he was taking.

Now Tallmadge became upset. He insisted that the messenger ride to West Point and contact Washington before Lieutenant Allen reached Arnold with Jameson's letter. The traitor would surely run when he received the letter if Washington did not first receive the news and arrest him.

Before the rider left, André decided he wanted to include a note with Jameson's letter. In his note, he confessed — perhaps none too wisely — that "the person in your possession is Major John André, Adjutant General of the British Army."

With André's confession, Arnold's treason was out in the open. But only two men knew about it: Tallmadge and Jameson. As the day wore on and Monday came, both men wondered which rider would win and who — Washington or Arnold — would learn first that the plot had been discovered.

Flight to the *Vulture*

The Arnolds were spending a quiet Monday morning. Peggy was still in her bedchamber. Two young officers had gone to a nearby orchard to fetch peaches for her and she was sitting up in bed awaiting her breakfast treat. The general was downstairs at the breakfast table chatting with Majors Samuel Shaw and James McHenry. They had arrived only moments before to announce that the commander in chief would be delayed and to start breakfast without him.

About ten o'clock, Lieutenant Solomon Allen, dusty and sweaty from his long ride, appeared with a letter from Lieutenant Colonel Jameson. Excusing himself, Arnold took the letter and broke the seal.

One can only imagine Arnold's shock, his disbelief, and then the chilling realization that his plot had been discovered. André taken! By now, even Washington must know of his dealings with the British.

Controlling himself, he told Allen to wait for an answer. Quickly he hobbled into the stable yard, ordered his horse saddled, and the pistols in the saddle holsters loaded. He sent a servant down to the river with orders for his barge to stand by.

Then, as fast as his bad leg would carry him, he went back to the house, through the dining room, and up the stairs to his wife's room. McHenry noticed Arnold. He was in an "embarrassment and agitation so unusual that I knew not to what to attribute it."

Arnold told Peggy of André's capture. But he had time for no more than a few hasty words. A knock sounded. His secretary, David Franks, called through the door that the commander in chief's two

[49]

servants had just arrived to report that "His Excellency is nigh at hand." Peggy fainted.

Arnold bolted from the room so fast that he almost knocked Franks down. He shouted that he was going to West Point to prepare a reception for Washington. Limping down the stairs and out to the stable yard, he leaped on his waiting horse, then immediately drew in on the reins. Around the corner of the stable appeared four of Washington's light horsemen. Arnold's hands went for his loaded pistols, but one of the officers saluted respectfully and said the commander in chief was coming up the road immediately behind them. So! Washington hadn't as yet received Jameson's letter. There was still time.

Arnold told the four to stable their horses and go into the house for breakfast. Then he galloped across the yard, down a sharp drop to the river, and reined up at his barge. He ordered the crew to row hard for Stony Point. He was in a hurry, he said, because he was "anxious to return to meet His Excellency."

At Stony Point, Arnold told the crew he had changed his mind. He now wanted to go to the *Vulture* where he had "particular business from His Excellency" with the *Vulture*'s captain.

The crew looked at each other. The *Vulture* was an enemy ship. Arnold saw their hesitation. Quickly he promised them two gallons of rum. At this offer, the prospect seemed brighter, but not for long.

As the barge bumped alongside the sloop of war, Arnold leaped over the rail, pulled pistols, and pointed them at the crew. He had recognized the failings of the rebel cause, he announced to the startled bargemen. He was returning to his rightful allegiance to the Crown and was now a British officer. They were, he declared, prisoners of war. Numbly, the barge crew climbed over the rail and were herded below.

[50]

Benedict Arnold boarding the Vulture. *(Charles Phelps Cushing)*

Arnold had changed sides definitely now. For better or worse, the act was done. Everything he owned — home, money, position, reputation — he had left behind some twelve miles up the Hudson.

The *Vulture* raised sail and headed downriver toward New York. Sir Henry, a little appalled at his new general's sense of fair play, ordered the barge crew released when the *Vulture* reached New York the next day.

The New British General

Arnold's treachery, it turned out, paid off handsomely. To make up for the loss of his personal property, Clinton awarded him

The house in Tappan, New York, where André was confined before his execution. (Charles Phelps Cushing)

The death warrant is read to Major André in this Chappel painting. André's reported reply was: "I am ready at any moment." (Charles Phelps Cushing)

£6,315. He was also commissioned a brigadier general which paid £650 annually. Two years later, King George awarded Peggy £500 a year for life.

While British officers were polite to Arnold, they tended nevertheless to avoid him. Many of these officers had been friends of André's and they held Arnold at least partly responsible for the young major's death.

The execution by hanging of Major John André, from a rare print published in Barnard's History of England. (Library of Congress)

André was convicted of being a spy and, on October 2, he was hanged at Tappan army camp. And, despite Clinton's public announcement about Arnold returning to his lawful position as a subject of the Crown, other officers did not accept this in their hearts. Arnold had fought honorably and well for five years for American independence, and then he had changed sides. He was a deserter, a traitor. Men of honor did not change sides.

Arnold took command of two expeditions for Sir Henry. On January 12, 1781, sixteen hundred men under his command attacked Richmond, Virginia. The redcoats drove civilians out of the city and fired homes, tobacco warehouses, and public buildings.

This block of granite on a hilltop in Tappan, New York, marks the place where Major André was hanged. "He was more unfortunate than criminal," George Washington is said to have declared. And he added: "An accomplished man and a gallant officer." (Charles Phelps Cushing)

In September of the same year, Arnold led another expedition up Long Island Sound to New London, Connecticut. The raid was actually a maneuver to divert the Americans from Yorktown where Cornwallis was boxed in. The raid ended with 140 homes, several ships, buildings, and warehouses being put to the torch. It was a grim, dirty business — not Arnold's former style of battle at all.

With Arnold to Richmond and New London went two lieutenant colonels to serve as his aides. The real function of these officers was to watch Arnold. They carried a "blank dormant commission," as Clinton called it. The officers could fill in their own names, date it, and suddenly outrank Arnold. The officers were to use the commission only if Arnold failed "to execute the duties of his command."

Although Arnold did not know it, he was being watched and guarded. His new friends simply did not trust him.

Toward the End

As Lord Cornwallis surrendered at Yorktown, the redcoats stacked their arms and marched between lines of rebels while a band played "The World Turned Upside Down." The unbelievable had happened; the rabble in the colonies, the farmboys turned soldiers, had defeated the mightiest army in the world.

A few weeks later, on December 15, 1781, Benedict Arnold boarded a transport in New York Harbor and sailed in a convoy of a hundred ships for England. He would never again return to what would soon become the United States of America.

If Arnold had fears about his reception in England, they were soon dispelled. He and Peggy were presented in court to King George III who treated them kindly. The king's brother and the Prince of Wales walked with Arnold in the public gardens. The Arnolds took a house in Portman Square and were accepted into society. "She was well dressed and had an ease in her behavior which astonished everybody," a friend of Clinton's wrote.

Although Arnold and Peggy did not realize it, they were novelties; everyone wanted to meet the famous American general and his wife. In time, the novelty wore off and Arnold and Peggy drifted into the background of court society. In time, they were forgotten.

Arnold bought a ship and resumed his old prewar occupation as a merchant. In 1785, he left London to establish his business in St. John, New Brunswick, in southeast Canada. There he built a home and a store, took in a business partner, and traded in lumber with the West Indies.

Yet, in one way, Arnold had not changed. He still had a way of attracting trouble. He was constantly harrassed by lawsuits. Men borrowed money from him and then refused to pay it back. A warehouse burned and he was accused by his partner of starting the fire, even though he was at sea when the fire broke out.

One night in 1791, a mob of former loyalists gathered outside his home, burned a straw figure of him, and shouted, "Traitor! Traitor!" Arnold was watching from behind the curtains of an upstairs bedroom. It was not a pleasant tribute from onetime Americans who had supported the Crown in the War for Independence.

Arnold returned to London in July, 1792, and wrote to Sir Henry with a request to rejoin the army. Clinton promised to do his best, but Arnold never heard from him again. In 1796, 1797, and 1799, he appealed directly to the government to get back into the army. Surely every experienced officer must be needed, for England was again at war with France. Yet each time his request went unanswered. The plain truth of the matter was that the army did not want him. When Arnold finally realized this, it broke his pride and health.

By 1800 his shipping ventures had lost money and he was near bankruptcy. He was forced to live on Peggy's £500 yearly pension. Their only friends were a few loyalists who lived in London.

In 1801, Arnold — now stooped and his flesh hanging loosely — developed a steady cough. His old leg wound from Bemis Heights ached worse than ever and he had to walk with a cane. By June, he developed dropsy (edema) in his crippled leg. His throat became inflamed; asthma was slowly choking him. At six thirty in the morning on June 12, Arnold died. His doctor said: "He expired without a groan."

Only two newspapers noted General Arnold's death. One of them, the *Morning Post*, reported on June 17th: "Poor General Arnold has departed this world without notice." It was true; few people remembered the brilliant battlefield officer from the American war of a quarter-century past.

Arnold's family buried him at St. Mary's, an ivy-covered church in Battersea on the banks of the Thames River. Three years later, Peggy joined her husband. The church and graveyard remain today, but the neighborhood has changed. The three sides of the graveyard are surrounded by a flour mill, small factories, and rundown tenements.

Selected Bibliography

Fleming, Thomas J. *West Point: The Men and Times of the United States Military Academy*. New York: William Morrow & Company, 1969.

Flexner, James Thomas. *The Traitor and the Spy*. New York: Harcourt, Brace, 1953.

Ford, Corey. *A Peculiar Service*. Boston: Little, Brown & Company, 1965.

Roberts, Kenneth. *March to Quebec*. New York: Doubleday, Doran & Company, 1938.

Van Doren, Carl. *Secret History of the American Revolution*. New York: Viking Press, 1941.

Wallace, Willard. *Traitorous Hero*. New York: Harper, 1954.

The Editors of American Heritage. *The American Heritage Book of the Revolution*. New York: American Heritage Publishing Company, 1958.

Selected readings from the Library of Congress, Washington, D.C.

Index

French army, 3, 29

Gates, General Horatio, 3, 12-13, 14, 15
George, Lake, 9, 31
George III, King, 53, 57
Germain, Lord George, 8
German soldiers, 11
Greene, General Nathanael, 8
Grey, Major General Charles, 25

Hamilton, Colonel Alexander, 5, 7
Hardscrabble Road, 41
Hartford, 3, 4, 31, 47, 48
Haverstraw Bay, 35
Howe, General Sir William, 11, 25
Hudson River, 3, 5, 6, 11, 27, 29, 31, 32,
  33, 34, 35, 37, 39, 40, 47, 50, 52

Jamaica, 37
Jameson, Lieutenant Colonel John, 7,
  46, 47, 48, 49
John Penn mansion, 17

Kennebec River, 9
King's Ferry, 31, 39
Kosciusko, Thaddeus, 33

Lafayette, Marquis de, 5, 7
Lamb, Colonel, 6
Lee, Richard Henry, 19, 20
Livingston, Colonel James, 40
London, 57, 58
Long Island Sound, 20, 56
Louis XVI, King, 15
Loyalists (Tories), 8, 18, 23, 25, 35, 57,
  58
Luzerne, Chevalier de la, 18

McDougall, Alexander, 33
McHenry, Major James, 5, 49
Maxwell, General William, 13

Mease, General James, 17
Montgomery, General Richard, 9, 10
Montreal, 9, 11
Morning Post, 58
Morristown, 3
Mount Pleasant, 21

Narragansett Bay, 3
New Brunswick, 57
Newburgh, 27
New England, 11, 32
New Haven, 9, 17
New London, 56
New York City, 4, 5, 7, 11, 18, 23, 34,
  38, 42, 43, 44, 47, 52, 56
New York State, 5, 35, 42
North Carolina, 4
North Castle, 7, 46, 47, 48
North River. *See* Hudson River
Norwich, 8

Old Southwark Theater, 18

Paoli Massacre, 25
Patriots, 8, 18
Paulding, John, 41, 42, 43, 46, 47
Peekskill, 31, 48
Pennsylvania, 25
Pennsylvania, Council of, 18, 19, 20
Philadelphia, 8, 16, 17, 18, 20, 23, 25, 27
Philadelphia, 12
Pine's Bridge, 41
Portman Square, 57
Providence, 8

Quebec, Battle of, 9-11
Quebec City, 9, 10

Redoubts (earthworks), 5, 14, 15, 37
Rhode Island, 29
Richmond, 55, 56

[62]

Robert Kraske became interested in Benedict Arnold nearly twenty years ago. Working in the Library of Congress one day, he came across little-known historical recollections on Arnold and his treason. From that beginning, he read everything available on the American Revolution's most talented battlefield commander. The present volume is his third book for young readers. Now living in Kettering, Ohio, Mr. Kraske is married and has three children. He is the editor of an education magazine for teachers.